This book belongs to:

________________________

7